Flying at Night

Pitt Poetry Series
Ed Ochester, Editor

Flying at Night

POEMS 1965–1985

Ted Kooser

UNIVERSITY OF PITTSBURGH PRESS

PENNSYLVANIA
COUNCIL
ON THE

ARTS

The publication of this
book is supported by a
grant from the
Pennsylvania Council
on the Arts

Published by the University of Pittsburgh Press,
Pittsburgh, PA 15260

Copyright © 1980, 1985, Ted Kooser

Manufactured in the United States of America

Printed on acid-free paper

10 9 8 7 6 5 4 3 2 1

ISBN 0-8229-4258-5 cloth / 0-8229-5877-5 paper

Contents

Sure Signs

Selecting a Reader

First, I would have her be beautiful,
and walking carefully up on my poetry
at the loneliest moment of an afternoon,
her hair still damp at the neck
from washing it. She should be wearing
a raincoat, an old one, dirty
from not having money enough for the cleaners.
She will take out her glasses, and there
in the bookstore, she will thumb
over my poems, then put the book back
up on its shelf. She will say to herself,
"For that kind of money, I can get
my raincoat cleaned." And she will.

First Snow

The old black dog comes in one evening
with the first few snowflakes on his back
and falls asleep, throwing his bad leg out
at our excitement. This is the night
when one of us gets to say, as if it were news,
that no two snowflakes are ever alike;
the night when each of us remembers something
snowier. The kitchen is a kindergarten
steamy with stories. The dog gets stiffly up
and limps away, seeking a quiet spot
at the heart of the house. Outside,
in silence, with diamonds in his fur,
the winter night curls round the legs of the trees,
sleepily blinking snowflakes from his lashes.

An Old Photograph

This old couple, Nils and Lydia,
were married for seventy years.
Here they are sixty years old
and already like brother
and sister—small, lustreless eyes,
large ears, the same serious line
to the mouths. After those years
spent together, sharing
the weather of sex, the sour milk
of lost children, barns burning,
grasshoppers, fevers and silence,
they were beginning to share
their hard looks. How far apart
they sit; not touching at shoulder
or knee, hands clasped in their laps
as if under each pair was a key
to a trunk hidden somewhere,
full of those lessons one keeps
to himself.
            They had probably
risen at daybreak, and dressed
by the stove, Lydia wearing
black wool with a collar of lace,
Nils his worn suit. They had driven
to town in the wagon and climbed
to the studio only to make
this stern statement, now veined
like a leaf, that though they looked
just alike they were separate people,
with separate wishes already
gone stale, a good two feet of space
between them, thirty years to go.

The Constellation Orion

I'm delighted to see you,
old friend,
lying there in your hammock
over the next town.
You were the first person
my son was to meet in the heavens.
He's sleeping now,
his head like a small sun in my lap.
Our car whizzes along in the night.
If he were awake, he'd say,
"Look, Daddy, there's Old Ryan!"
but I won't wake him.
He's mine for the weekend,
Old Ryan, not yours.

The Salesman

Today he's wearing his vinyl shoes,
shiny and white as little Karmann Ghias
fresh from the body shop, and as he moves
in his door-to-door glide, these shoes fly round
each other, honking the horns of their soles.
His hose are black and ribbed and tight, as thin
as an old umbrella or the wing of a bat.
(They leave a pucker when he pulls them off.)
He's got on his double-knit leisure suit
in a pond-scum green, with a tight white belt
that matches his shoes but suffers with cracks
at the golden buckle. His shirt is brown
and green, like a pile of leaves, and it opens
onto the neck at a Brillo pad
of graying hair which tosses a cross and chain
as he walks. The collar is splayed out over
the jacket's lapels yet leaves a lodge pin
taking the sun like a silver spike.
He's swinging a briefcase full of the things
of this world, a leather cornucopia
heavy with promise. Through those dark lenses,
each of the doors along your sunny street
looks slightly ajar, and in your quiet house
the dog of your willpower cowers and growls,
then crawls in under the basement steps,
making the jingle of coin with its tags.

Old Soldiers' Home

On benches in front of the Old Soldiers' Home,
the old soldiers unwrap the pale brown packages
of their hands, folding the fingers back
and looking inside, then closing them up again
and gazing off across the grounds,
safe with the secret.

Self-Portrait at Thirty-Nine

A barber is cutting the hair;
his fingers, perfumed by a rainbow
of bottled oils, blanket the head
with soft, pink clouds. Through these,
the green eyes, from their craters, peer.

There's a grin lost somewhere
in the folds of the face, with a fence
of old teeth, broken and leaning,
through which asides to the barber
pounce catlike onto the air.

This is a face which shows its age,
has all of the coin it started with,
with the look of having been counted
too often. Oh, but I love
my face! It is that hound of bronze

who faithfully stands by the door
to hold it open wide—on light,
on water, on leafy streets
where women pass it with a smile.
Good dog, old face; good dog, good dog.

Christmas Eve

Now my father carries his old heart
in its basket of ribs
like a child coming into the room
with an injured bird.
Our ages sit down with a table between them,
eager to talk.
Our common bones are wrapped in new robes.
A common pulse tugs at the ropes
in the backs of our hands.
We are so much alike
we both weep at the end of his stories.

Visiting Mountains

The plains ignore us,
but these mountains listen,
an audience of thousands
holding its breath
in each rock. Climbing,
we pick our way
over the skulls of small talk.
On the prairies below us,
the grass leans this way and that
in discussion;
words fly away like corn shucks
over the fields.
Here, lost in a mountain's
attention, there's nothing to say.

The Leaky Faucet

All through the night, the leaky faucet
searches the stillness of the house
with its radar blip: who is awake?
Who lies out there as full of worry
as a pan in the sink? *Cheer up,*
cheer up, the little faucet calls,
someone will help you through your life.

A Frozen Stream

This snake has gone on,
all muscle and glitter,
into the woods,
a few leaves clinging,
red, yellow, and brown.
Oh, how he sparkled!
The roots of the old trees
gleamed as he passed.

Now there is nothing
to see; an old skin
caught in the bushes,
bleached and flaking,
a few sharp stones
already poking through.

Living Near the Rehabilitation Home

Tonight she is making her way
up the block by herself, throwing
her heavy shoes from step to step,
her lunchbox swinging out wide
with a rhythmical clunk, each bone
on its end and feebly bending
into her pitiful gait. Where is
her friend tonight, the idiot boy?
Each day at this time I see them
walking together, his bright red jacket
trying the dusk, her old blue coat
his shadow. She moves too slowly
for him, and he breaks from her hand
and circles her in serious orbits,
stamping his feet in the grass.
Perhaps they have taken him elsewhere
to live. From high on my good legs
I imagine her lonely without him,
but perhaps she's happy at last.

Late February

The first warm day,
and by mid-afternoon
the snow is no more
than a washing
strewn over the yards,
the bedding rolled in knots
and leaking water,
the white shirts lying
under the evergreens.
Through the heaviest drifts
rise autumn's fallen
bicycles, small carnivals
of paint and chrome,
the Octopus
and Tilt-A-Whirl
beginning to turn
in the sun. Now children,
stiffened by winter
and dressed, somehow,
like old men, mutter
and bend to the work
of building dams.

But such a spring is brief;
by five o'clock
the chill of sundown,
darkness, the blue TVs
flashing like storms
in the picture windows,
the yards gone gray,
the wet dogs barking
at nothing. Far off

across the cornfields
staked for streets and sewers,
the body of a farmer
missing since fall
will show up
in his garden tomorrow,
as unexpected
as a tulip.

A Drive in the Country

In the ditch by the dirt back road
late in March, a few black snowdrifts
lie in the grass like old men
asleep in their coats. It's the dirt
of the road that has kept them
so cold at the heart. We drive by
without stopping for them.

Spring Plowing

West of Omaha the freshly plowed fields
steam in the night like lakes.
The smell of the earth floods over the roads.
The field mice are moving their nests
to the higher ground of fence rows,
the old among them crying out to the owls
to take them all. The paths in the grass
are loud with the squeak of their carts.
They keep their lanterns covered.

Sitting All Evening Alone in the Kitchen

The cat has fallen asleep,
the dull book of a dead moth
loose in his paws.

The moon in the window, the tide
gurgling out through the broken shells
in the old refrigerator.

Late, I turn out the lights.
The little towns on top of the stove
glow faintly neon,
sad women alone at the bar.

Sure Signs

—for George Von Glahn

So many crickets tonight—
like strings of sleigh bells!
"A long hard winter ahead
for sure," my neighbor says,
reeling a cobweb onto
a broom in his garden.
"Crickets and cobwebs," he says,
"sure signs. In seventy years
(he looks out over his glasses
to see if I'm still there)
you get to know a thing or two."

A Summer Night

At the end of the street
a porch light is burning,
showing the way. How simple,
how perfect it seems: the darkness,
the white house like a passage
through summer and into
a snowfield. Night after night,
the lamp comes on at dusk,
the end of the street
stands open and white,
and an old woman sits there
tending the lonely gate.

In a Country Cemetery in Iowa

—*for James Hearst*

Someone's been up here nights,
and in a hurry,
breaking the headstones.

And someone else,
with a little time to spare,
has mended them;

some farmer, I'd say,
who knows his welding.
He's stacked them up in

harnesses of iron,
old angle iron and strap,
taking a little extra time

to file the welds down smooth.
Just passing through, you'd say
it looks like foolishness.

The Man with the Hearing Aid

A man takes out his hearing aid
and falls asleep, his good ear deep
in the pillow. Thousands of bats
fly out of the other ear.
All night they flutter and dive
through laughter, catching the punch lines,
their ears all blood and velvet.
At dawn they return. The weary squeaks
make the old stone cavern ring
with gibberish. As the man awakens,
the last of the bats folds into sleep.
His ear is thick with fur and silence.

The Very Old

The very old are forever
hurting themselves,

burning their fingers
on skillets, falling

loosely as trees
and breaking their hips

with muffled explosions of bone.
Down the block

they are wheeled in
out of our sight

for years at a time.
To make conversation,

the neighbors ask
if they are still alive.

Then, early one morning,
through our kitchen windows

we see them again,
first one and then another,

out in their gardens
on crutches and canes,

perennial,
checking their gauges for rain.

Walking Beside a Creek

Walking beside a creek
in December, the black ice
windy with leaves,
you can feel the great joy
of the trees, their coats
thrown open like drunken men,
the lifeblood thudding
in their tight, wet boots.

Book Club

Mother has come to the clean end
of a morning full of the clink of mints
in little dishes, of lemon oil
tart in the living-room air,
of the water ballet of the folding chairs
rehearsing their kicks in a circle
of patience. The ladies are due
at two o'clock, a fat tour guide
of Hawaii on schedule, lagoons
of romance to lap the hot shore
in each girdle, volcanoes of ashes
filling the ashtrays, the bright birds
of sweet smiles crisscrossing
the circle.
        Meanwhile, my father
is picking up leaves from the drive;
as he bends, his blood tries the loose doors
of his arteries. At sixty-six,
with his retirement Bulova
wound tight as his heart, he has entered
the blue, high-altitude hallway of age.
There air is thin. If he looks forward
or back he gets dizzy. Today, in the bleak
exile of book club, even his bathroom's
forbidden to him. His razor and soap
have been hidden, his pills put away.

If he needs to go to the bathroom,
he'll have to walk down to the station
and ask for the key. Most likely though,

he's safe.
                    At the foot of the stairs
to the basement, he's drawn up an armchair
and floor lamp. Through the long afternoon,
he'll sit there pretending to read,
while above him the pink mints go around
in slow circles, and lovely Hawaii
comes to Des Moines in the hula
of numb fannies on laboring chairs.

At the End of the Weekend

It is Sunday afternoon,
and I suddenly miss
my distant son, who at ten
has just this instant buzzed
my house in a flying
cardboard box, dipping
one wing to look down over
my shimmering roof, the yard,
the car in the drive. In his room
three hundred miles from me,
he tightens his helmet,
grips the controls, turns
loops and rolls. My windows
rattle. On days like this,
the least quick shadow crossing
the page makes me look up
at the sky like a goose,
squinting to see that flash
that I dream is his thought of me
daring to fall through the distance,
then climbing, full throttle, away.

Uncle Adler

He had come to the age
when his health had put cardboard
in all of its windows.
The oil in his eyes was so old
it would barely light,
and his chest was a chimney
full of bees. Of it all,
he had nothing to say;
his Adam's apple hung like a ham
in a stairwell. Lawyers
encircled the farm like a fence,
and his daughters fought over
the china. Then one day
while everyone he'd ever loved
was digging in his yard,
he suddenly sucked in his breath so hard
the whole estate fell in on him.

In the Corners of Fields

Something is calling to me
from the corners of fields,
where the leftover fence wire
suns its loose coils, and stones
thrown out of the furrow
sleep in warm litters;
where the gray faces
of old No Hunting signs
mutter into the wind,
and dry horse tanks
spout fountains of sunflowers;
where a moth
flutters in from the pasture,
harried by sparrows,
and alights on a post,
so sure of its life
that it peacefully opens its wings.

How to Make Rhubarb Wine

Go to the patch some afternoon
in early summer, fuzzy with beer
and sunlight, and pick a sack
of rhubarb (red or green will do)
and God knows watch for rattlesnakes
or better, listen; they make a sound
like an old lawn mower rolled downhill.
Wear a hat. A straw hat's best
for the heat but lets the gnats in.
Bunch up the stalks and chop the leaves off
with a buck knife and be careful.
You need ten pounds; a grocery bag
packed full will do it. Then go home
and sit barefooted in the shade
behind the house with a can of beer.
Spread out the rhubarb in the grass
and wash it with cold water
from the garden hose, washing
your feet as well. Then take a nap.
That evening, dice the rhubarb up
and put it in a crock. Then pour
eight quarts of boiling water in,
cover it up with a checkered cloth
to keep the fruit flies out of it,
and let it stand five days or so.
Take time each day to think of it.

Ferment ten days, under the cloth,
sniffing of it from time to time,
then siphon it off, swallowing some,

and bottle it. Sit back and watch
the liquid clear to honey yellow,
bottled and ready for the years,
and smile. You've done it awfully well.

Late Lights in Minnesota

At the end of a freight train rolling away,
a hand swinging a lantern.
The only lights left behind in the town
are a bulb burning cold in the jail,
and high in one house,
a five-battery flashlight
pulling an old woman downstairs to the toilet
among the red eyes of her cats.

The Afterlife

It will be February there,
a foreign-language newspaper
rolling along the dock
in an icy wind, a few
old winos wiping their eyes
over a barrel of fire;
down the streets, mad women
shaking rats from their mops
on each stoop, and odd,
twisted children,
playing with matches and knives.
Then, behind us, trombones:
the horns of the tugs
turning our great gray ship
back into the mist.

A Widow

She's combed his neckties out of her hair
and torn out the tongues of his shoes.
She's poured his ashes out of their urn
and into his humidor. For the very last time,
she's scrubbed the floor around the toilet.
She hates him even more for dying.

So This Is Nebraska

The gravel road rides with a slow gallop
over the fields, the telephone lines
streaming behind, its billow of dust
full of the sparks of redwing blackbirds.

On either side, those dear old ladies,
the loosening barns, their little windows
dulled by cataracts of hay and cobwebs
hide broken tractors under their skirts.

So this is Nebraska. A Sunday
afternoon; July. Driving along
with your hand out squeezing the air,
a meadowlark waiting on every post.

Behind a shelterbelt of cedars,
top-deep in hollyhocks, pollen and bees,
a pickup kicks its fenders off
and settles back to read the clouds.

You feel like that; you feel like letting
your tires go flat, like letting the mice
build a nest in your muffler, like being
no more than a truck in the weeds,

clucking with chickens or sticky with honey
or holding a skinny old man in your lap
while he watches the road, waiting
for someone to wave to. You feel like

waving. You feel like stopping the car
and dancing around on the road. You wave
instead and leave your hand out gliding
larklike over the wheat, over the houses.

Fort Robinson

When I visited Fort Robinson,
where Dull Knife and his Northern Cheyenne
were held captive that terrible winter,
the grounds crew was killing the magpies.

Two men were going from tree to tree
with sticks and ladders, poking the young birds
down from their nests and beating them to death
as they hopped about in the grass.

Under each tree where the men had worked
were twisted clots of matted feathers,
and above each tree a magpie circled,
crazily calling in all her voices.

We didn't get out of the car.
My little boy hid in the back and cried
as we drove away, into those ragged buttes
the Cheyenne climbed that winter, fleeing.

How to Foretell a Change in the Weather

Rain always follows the cattle
sniffing the air and huddling
in fields with their heads to the lee.
You will know that the weather is changing
when your sheep leave the pasture
too slowly, and your dogs lie about
and look tired; when the cat
turns her back to the fire,
washing her face, and the pigs
wallow in litter; cocks will be crowing
at unusual hours, flapping their wings;
hens will chant; when your ducks
and your geese are too noisy,
and the pigeons are washing themselves;
when the peacocks squall loudly
from the tops of the trees,
when the guinea fowl grates;
when sparrows chip loudly
and fuss in the roadway, and when swallows
fly low, skimming the earth;
when the carrion crow
croaks to himself, and wild fowl
dip and wash, and when moles
throw up hills with great fervor;
when toads creep out in numbers;
when frogs croak; when bats
enter the houses; when birds
begin to seek shelter,
and the robin approaches your house;
when the swan flies at the wind,

and your bees leave the hive;
when ants carry their eggs to and fro,
and flies bite, and the earthworm
is seen on the surface of things.

Snow Fence

The red fence
takes the cold trail
north; no meat
on its ribs,
but neither has it
much to carry.

In an Old Apple Orchard

The wind's an old man
to this orchard; these trees
have been feeling
the soft tug of his gloves
for a hundred years.
Now it's April again,
and again that old fool
thinks he's young.
He's combed the dead leaves
out of his beard; he's put on
perfume. He's gone off
late in the day
toward the town, and come back
slow in the morning,
reeling with bees.
As late as noon, if you look
in the long grass,
you can see him
still rolling about in his sleep.

An Empty Place

There is nothing for Death
in an empty house,
nor left for him in the white dish
broken over the road.

Come and sit down by me
on the sunny stoop,
and let your heart so gently
rock you, rock you.

There is nothing to harm us here.

After the Funeral:
Cleaning Out the Medicine Cabinet

Behind this mirror no new world
opens to Alice. Instead, we find
the old world, rearranged in rows,
a dusty little chronicle
of small complaints and private sorrows,
each cough caught dry and airless
in amber, the sore feet powdered
and cool in their yellow can.
To this world turned the burning eyes
after their search, the weary back
after its lifting, the heavy heart
like an old dog, sniffing the lid
for an answer. Now one of us
unscrews the caps and tries the air
of each disease. Another puts
the booty in a shoe box: tins
of laxatives and aspirin,
the corn pads and the razor blades,
while still another takes the vials
of secret sorrows—the little pills
with faded, lonely codes—holding
them out the way one holds a spider
pinched in a tissue, and pours them down
the churning toilet and away.

The Grandfather Cap

Sometimes I think that as he aged,
this cap, with the stain in its brim
like a range of dark mountains,
became the horizon to him.
He never felt right with it off.

Shooting a Farmhouse

The first few wounds are nearly invisible;
a truck rumbles past in the dust
and a .22 hole appears in the mailbox
like a fly landing there.
In a month you can see sky
through the tail of the windmill.
The attic windows grow black and uneasy.
When the last hen is found shot in the yard,
the old man and his wife move away.

In November, a Land Rover
flattens the gate like a tank
and pulls up in the yard. Hunters spill out
and throw down their pheasants like hats.
They blow out the rest of the windows,
set beer cans up on the porch rails
and shoot from the hip.
One of them walks up and yells in,
"Is anyone home?" getting a laugh.

By sunset, they've kicked down the door.
In the soft blush of light,
they blast holes in the plaster
and piss on the floors.

When the beer and the shells are all gone,
they drive sadly away,
the blare of their radio fading.
A breeze sighs in the shelterbelt.
Back in the house,

the newspapers left over from packing
the old woman's dishes
begin to blow back and forth through the rooms.

Beer Bottle

In the burned-
out highway
ditch the throw-

away beer
bottle lands
standing up

unbroken,
like a cat
thrown off

of a roof
to kill it,
landing hard

and dazzled
in the sun,
right side up;

sort of a
miracle.

Sleeping Cat

My cat is asleep on his haunches
like a sphinx. He has gone down cautiously
into an earlier life, holding a thread
of the old world's noises, and feeling his way
through the bones. The scratch of my pen
keeps the thread taut. When I finish
the poem, and the sound in the room goes slack,
the cat will come scampering back
into the blinding, bright rooms of his eyes.

North of Alliance

This is an empty house; not a stick
of furniture left, not even
a newspaper sodden with rain
under a broken window; nothing
to tell us the style of the people
who lived here, but that
they took it along. But wait:
here, penciled in inches
up a doorframe, these little marks
mark the growth of a child
impatient to get on with it,
a child stretching his neck
in a hurry to leave nothing here
but an absence grown tall in a doorway.

Late September

Behind each garage a ladder
sleeps in the leaves, its hands
folded across its lean belly.
There are hundreds of them
in each town, and more
sleeping by haystacks and barns
out in the country—tough old
day laborers, seasoned and wheezy,
drunk on the weather,
sleeping outside with the crickets.

Carrie

"There's never an end to dust
and dusting," my aunt would say
as her rag, like a thunderhead,
scudded across the yellow oak
of her little house. There she lived
seventy years with a ball
of compulsion closed in her fist,
and an elbow that creaked and popped
like a branch in a storm. Now dust
is her hands and dust her heart.
There's never an end to it.

For a Friend

Late November, driving to Wichita.
A black veil of starlings
snags on a thicket and falls.
Shadows of wings skitter over
the highway, like leaves, like ashes.

You have been dead for six months;
though summer and fall
were lighter by one life,
they didn't seem to show it.
The seasons, those steady horses,
are used to the fickle weight
of our shifting load.

I'll guess how it was; on the road
through the wood, you stood up
in the back of the hangman's cart,
reached a low-hanging branch,
and swung up into the green leaves
of our memories.
                        Old friend,
the stars were shattered windshield glass
for weeks; we all were sorry.

They never found that part of you
that made you drink, that made you cruel.
You knew we loved you anyway.

Black streak across the centerline,
all highways make me think of you.

Grandfather

Driving the team, he came up over
the hill and looked down. In the white bowl
of the snow-covered valley, his house
was aflame like a wick, drawing up
into itself all that he'd worked for.

Once, forty years later, we passed.
It was October. The cellar
was filled by a flame of young trees.
I got out, but he sat in the back
and stared straight ahead, this old, old man,
still tight on the reins of his years.

Looking for You, Barbara

I have been out looking for you,
Barbara, and as I drove around,
the steering wheel turned through my hands
like a clock. The moon
rolled over the rooftops and was gone.

I was dead tired; in my arms
they were rolling the tires inside;
in my legs they were locking the pumps.
Yet what was in me for you
flapped as red in my veins
as banners strung over a car lot.

Then I came home and got drunk.
Where were you? 2 A.M.
is full of slim manikins
waving their furs from black windows.
My bed goes once more around the block,
and my heart keeps on honking its horn.

Pocket Poem

If this comes creased and creased again and soiled
as if I'd opened it a thousand times
to see if what I'd written here was right,
it's all because I looked for you too long
to put it in your pocket. Midnight says
the little gifts of loneliness come wrapped
by nervous fingers. What I wanted this
to say was that I want to be so close
that when you find it, it is warm from me.

Moles

The young of the mole
are born in the skull of a mayor.
They learn *footfall*
and *rain*. In the Season
of Falling Pinecones, they gather
in churches of ribs,
whining and puking.
When one of the old moles dies,
the young push him out of his tunnel
and set him afloat on the light.
This is the way we find them
out in the garden,
their little oars
pulled up and drying.

Notes on the Death of
Nels Paulssen, Farmer,
at the Ripe Old Age of 93

A harvest
of nail parings,

a wagonload
of hair—

over his ashen
fields,

no dust
in the air.

Advice

We go out of our way to get home,
getting lost in a rack of old clothing,
fainting in stairwells,
our pulses fluttering like moths.
We will always be
leaving our loves like old stoves
in abandoned apartments. Early in life
there are signals of how it will be—
we throw up the window one spring
and the window weights break from their ropes
and fall deep in the wall.

After My Grandmother's Funeral

After my grandmother's funeral,
as the dark river of mourners
murmured beneath me, I lay
on the floor of her attic,
watching the afternoon light
fade from the vault of old rafters
and dim to a film of gray dust
on her dresses and shoes.
I closed my eyes and slept,
but no dream came to me;
the coffin of that attic
was not to be borne aloft
on the good shoulders of cousins;
nor was it to roll on chrome wheels
to an altar with candles;
nor was I to awaken to find
my fingers laced loosely
over my heart. No dream came then
to help me leap over
the years to my death.
I awakened still young,
still sad, no longer welcome
in that darkening house.

A Hot Night in Wheat Country

One doctor in a Piper Cub
can wake up everyone in North Dakota.

At the level of an open upstairs window,
a great white plain stretches away—
the naked Methodists
lying on top of their bedding.

The moon covers her eyes with a cloud.

Five P.M.

The pigeon flies to her resting place
on a window ledge above the traffic,
and her shadow, which cannot fly, climbs
swiftly over the bricks to meet her there.

Just so are you and I gathered at 5:00,
your bicycle left by the porch, the wind
still ringing in it, and my shoes by the bed,
still warm from walking home to you.

Abandoned Farmhouse

He was a big man, says the size of his shoes
on a pile of broken dishes by the house;
a tall man too, says the length of the bed
in an upstairs room; and a good, God-fearing man,
says the Bible with a broken back
on the floor below the window, dusty with sun;
but not a man for farming, say the fields
cluttered with boulders and the leaky barn.

A woman lived with him, says the bedroom wall
papered with lilacs and the kitchen shelves
covered with oilcloth, and they had a child,
says the sandbox made from a tractor tire.
Money was scarce, say the jars of plum preserves
and canned tomatoes sealed in the cellar hole.
And the winters cold, say the rags in the window frames.
It was lonely here, says the narrow country road.

Something went wrong, says the empty house
in the weed-choked yard. Stones in the fields
say he was not a farmer; the still-sealed jars
in the cellar say she left in a nervous haste.
And the child? Its toys are strewn in the yard
like branches after a storm—a rubber cow,
a rusty tractor with a broken plow,
a doll in overalls. Something went wrong, they say.

The Blind Always Come as Such a Surprise

The blind always come as such a surprise,
suddenly filling an elevator
with a great white porcupine of canes,
or coming down upon us in a noisy crowd
like the eye of a hurricane.
The dashboards of cars stopped at crosswalks
and the shoes of commuters on trains
are covered with sentences
struck down in mid-flight by the canes of the blind.
Each of them changes our lives,
tapping across the bright circles of our ambitions
like cracks traversing the favorite china.

Furnace

There's a click like a piece of chalk
tapping a blackboard, and the furnace
starts thinking: *Now, just where was I?*
It's always the same stale thought
turned over and over: *Got to
get something to eat.* Nothing else
ever enters its mind. After all,
it's a very old furnace,
and all of its friends have moved on.

West Window

An owl
washes his claws
in the wind,
sets down
in light
no brighter
than a candle makes,
to eat. The days
draw back their warmth
from us
like cooling lamps.
We grow
to be alone
with table and cup.

Boarding House

The blind man draws his curtains for the night
and goes to bed, leaving a burning light

above the bathroom mirror. Through the wall,
he hears the deaf man walking down the hall

in his squeaky shoes to see if there's a light
under the blind man's door, and all is right.

A Letter from Aunt Belle

You couldn't have heard about it there—
I'll send the clippings later on.

The afternoon that the neighbors' stove exploded—
how it reminded me of . . . Sarah's garden wedding!
Do you remember? It was beautiful.

As I was watering those slips
I promised you—the violets—
there was an awful thud, and Samson's wall
puffed up and blew the windows out.
It turned some pictures in the living room,
and that lovely vase you children gave to me
Christmas of '56 fell down, but I can glue it.

That Franklin boy you knew in school—
the one who got that girl in trouble—
ran in the Samsons' house, but she was dead;
the blast collapsed her lungs, poor thing.
She always made me think of you,
but on the stretcher with her hair pinned up
and one old sandal off, she looked as old
as poor old me.
                            I have to go—
I've baked a little coffee cake
for Mr. Samson and the boys.

The violet slips are ready—
                                            Write.

At the Bait Stand

Part barn, part boxcar, part of a chicken shed,
part leaking water, something partly dead,
part pop machine, part gas pump, part a chair
leaned back against the wall, and sleeping there,
part-owner Herman Runner, mostly fat,
hip-waders, undershirt, tattoos and hat.

The Tattooed Lady

Around the smallpox vaccination scar
I'd hated since I was a little girl
I had him put this daisy, then its stem
because the flower looked too spidery
without a stem, and then these little leaves.
He said to think of it as just a gift
for a pretty girl. I went to him that night
because my arm was swollen, and I stayed
for twenty years. Around the daisy's stem
he slowly wound a snake that circled me
with swirls of trailer camps and cheap hotels
and sideshows, yet I loved the masterpiece
that I became to him. His touch had touched
me everywhere. His love is here to see.

A Death at the Office

The news goes desk to desk
like a memo: *Initial
and pass on.* Each of us marks
Surprised or *Sorry.*

The management came early
and buried her nameplate
deep in her desk. They have boxed up
the Midol and Lip-Ice,

the snapshots from home,
wherever it was—nephews
and nieces, a strange, blurred cat
with fiery, flashbulb eyes

as if it grieved. But who grieves here?
We have her ballpoints back,
her bud vase. One of us tears
the scribbles from her calendar.

There Is Always a Little Wind

There is always a little wind
in a country cemetery,
even on days when the air stands
still as a barn in the fields.

You can see the old cedars,
stringy and tough as maiden aunts,
taking the little gusts of wind
in their aprons like sheaves of wheat,

and hear above you the warm
and regular sweep of wheat being cut
and gathered, the wagons creaking,
the young men breathing at their work.

The Widow Lester

I was too old to be married,
but nobody told me.
I guess they didn't care enough.
How it had hurt, though, catching bouquets
all those years!
Then I met Ivan, and kept him,
and never knew love.
How his feet stunk in the bed sheets!
I could have told him to wash,
but I wanted to hold that stink against him.
The day he dropped dead in the field,
I was watching.
I was hanging up sheets in the yard,
and I finished.

Houses at the Edge of Town

These are the houses of farmers
retired from their fields;
white houses, freshly folded
and springing open again
like legal papers. These are houses
drawn up on the shore of the fields,
their nets still wet,
the fishermen sleeping curled in the bows.
See how the gardens
wade into the edge of the hayfield,
the cucumbers crawling out under the lilacs
to lie in the sun.

The Old Woman

The old woman, asleep on her back,
pulls up her knees and gives birth
to an empty house. She kicks off
the quilt and sheet and rakes her shift
up over her hips, showing her sex
to the photos of children
arranged on the opposite wall
who, years before, turned their
moonlit faces away.

A Place in Kansas

—for Jon Gierlich

Somewhere in Kansas, a friend found
an empty stone house alone in a wheatfield.
Over the door was incised a ship's anchor.
There was no one to ask
what that anchor was doing in Kansas,
no water for miles.
Not a single white sail of a meaning
broke the horizon, though he stood there for hours.
It's like that in Kansas, forever.

Tom Ball's Barn

—*for Bill Kloefkorn*

The loan that built the barn
just wasn't big enough
to buy the paint, so the barn
went bare and fell apart
at the mortgaged end of twelve
nail-popping, splintering winters.
Besides the Januaries,
the barber says it was
five-and-a-half percent,
three dry years, seven wet,
and two indifferent,
the banker (dead five years),
and the bank (still open
but deaf, or *deef* as it were), *and*
poor iron in the nails that
were all to blame for the barn's collapse
on everything he owned, thus
leading poor Tom's good health
to diabetes and
the swollen leg that threw him
off the silo, probably
dead (the doctor said)
before he hit that board pile.

My Grandfather Dying

I could see bruises or shadows
deep under his skin, like the shapes
skaters find frozen in rivers—
leaves caught in flight,
or maybe the hand of a man reaching up
out of the darkness for help.

I was helpless as flowers
there at his bedside. I watched
his legs jerk in the sheets.
He answered doors,
he kicked loose stones from his fields.
I leaned down to call out my name
and he called it back. His breath
was as sour as an orchard
after the first frost.

The Red Wing Church

There's a tractor in the doorway of a church
in Red Wing, Nebraska, in a coat of mud
and straw that drags the floor. A broken plow
sprawls beggarlike behind it on some planks
that make a sort of roadway up the steps.
The steeple's gone. A black tar-paper scar
that lightning might have made replaces it.
They've taken it down to change the house of God
to Homer Johnson's barn, but it's still a church,
with clumps of tiger lilies in the grass
and one of those boxlike, glassed-in signs
that give the sermon's topic (reading now
a bird's nest and a little broken glass).
The good works of the Lord are all around:
the steeple top is standing in a garden
just up the alley; it's a hen house now:
fat leghorns gossip at its crowded door.
Pews stretch on porches up and down the street,
the stained-glass windows style the mayor's house,
and the bell's atop the firehouse in the square.
The cross is only God knows where.

Highway 30

At two in the morning, when the moon
has driven away,
leaving the faint taillight of one star
at the horizon, a light
like moonlight leaks
from broken crates that lie fallen
along the highway, becoming
motels, all-night cafes, and bus stations
with greenhouse windows,
where lone women sit like overturned flowerpots,
crushing the soft, gray petals of old coats.

Birthday

Somebody deep in my bones
is lacing his shoes with a hook.
It's an hour before dawn
in that nursing home.
There is nothing to do but get dressed
and sit in the darkness.
Up the hall, in the brightly lit skull,
the young pastor is writing his poem.

The Failed Suicide

You have come back to us windblown
and wild-eyed, your fingertips numb
from squeezing the handle grips
of a four-day coma. Somehow,
out in that darkened countryside,
the road grew circular
and brought you back. We seem
another city, but the street signs
keep spelling your name, the same gnats
keep clouding the lights
high over the empty parking lots,
and the clock on the funeral home
(always a few minutes fast)
shines down upon a little fountain
where, nestled in curls of dead leaves,
a stone frog the color of your brain
prepares his leap.

The Goldfish Floats to the Top of His Life

The goldfish floats to the top of his life
and turns over, a shaving from somebody's hobby.
So it is that men die at the whims of great companies,
their neckties pulling them speechless into machines,
their wives finding them slumped in the shower,
their hearts blown open like boiler doors.
In the night, again and again these men float
to the tops of their dreams to drift back
to their desks in the morning. If you ask them,
they all would prefer to have died in their sleep.

They Had Torn Off My Face at the Office

They had torn off my face at the office.
The night that I finally noticed
that it was not growing back, I decided
to slit my wrists. Nothing ran out;
I was empty. Both of my hands fell off
shortly thereafter. Now at my job
they allow me to type with the stumps.
It pleases them to have helped me,
and I gain in speed and confidence.

Year's End

Now the seasons are closing their files
on each of us, the heavy drawers
full of certificates rolling back
into the tree trunks, a few old papers
flocking away. Someone we loved
has fallen from our thoughts,
making a little, glittering splash
like a bicycle pushed by a breeze.
Otherwise, not much has happened;
we fell in love again, finding
that one red feather on the wind.

New Year's Day

Each thing in the clean morning light
is a promise. I start the day
by building a feeding place for the birds,
stacking up castaway crates in the snow.
How they come! Sparrows and blue jays
dropping like leaves from the elms,
which though burned with disease
still promise some sort of a spring,
their branches lined with hard buds
like birds perching, or the seeds of birds,
still more birds to come.

Walking to Work

Today, it's the obsidian
ice on the sidewalk
with its milk white bubbles
popping under my shoes
that pleases me, and upon it
a lump of old snow
with a trail like a comet,
that somebody,
probably falling in love,
has kicked
all the way to the corner.

Sunday Morning

Now it is June again, one of those
leafy Sundays drifting through galaxies
of maple seeds. Somewhere, a mourning dove
touches her keyboard twice, a lonely F,
and then falls silent. Here in the house
the Sunday papers lie in whitecaps
over the living-room floor. Among them floats
the bridal page, that window of many panes,
reflecting, black and white, patches of sky
and puffs of starlit cloud becoming
faces. On each bright brow the same light falls,
the nuptial moon held up just out of sight
to the left. The brides all lift their eyes
and smile to see the heavens stopped for them.
And love is everywhere. Cars that have all week
lurched and honked with sour commuters are now
like smooth canoes packed soft with families.
A church bell strides through the green perfume
of locust trees and tolls its thankfulness.
The mourning dove, to her astonishment,
blunders upon a distant call in answer.

One World
at a Time

Flying at Night

Above us, stars. Beneath us, constellations.
Five billion miles away, a galaxy dies
like a snowflake falling on water. Below us,
some farmer, feeling the chill of that distant death,
snaps on his yard light, drawing his sheds and barn
back into the little system of his care.
All night, the cities, like shimmering novas,
tug with bright streets at lonely lights like his.

A Fencerow in Early March

The last snowdrifts
have drawn themselves up
out of the light,
clinging to winter.
Beyond them,
a muddy stubble field
has sponged up
all the darkness—
the February nights,
the iron stoves,
the ink of every letter
written in longing.
And the fencerow
goes on, up and over
the next low rise
and the next, casting
a cold, white shadow,
each gate still closed
to spring.

Just Now

Just now, if I look back down
the cool street of the past, I can see
streetlamps, one for each year,
lighting small circles of time
into which someone will step
if I squint, if I try hard enough—
circles smaller and smaller,
leading back to the one faint point
at the start, like a star.
So many of them are empty now,
those circles of roadside and grass.
In one, the moth of some feeling
still flutters, unspoken,
the cold darkness around it enormous.

A Birthday Card

In her eighties now, and weak and ill
with emphysema, my aunt sends me
a birthday card—a tossing ocean
with clipper ship—and wishes me
well at forty-four. She's included
a note—hard-bitten in ball-point,
with a pen that sometimes skips whole words
but never turns back—to tell me
her end of the news: how the steroids
have softened her spine, and now how
every x-ray shows more shattered bone.
Her hasty words skip in and out,
their little grooves washed clean of ink,
the message rising and falling
like short-wave radio, sending
this hurried SOS, with love.

In the Basement of the Goodwill Store

In musty light, in the thin brown air
of damp carpet, doll heads and rust,
beneath long rows of sharp footfalls
like nails in a lid, an old man stands
trying on glasses, lifting each pair
from the box like a glittering fish
and holding it up to the light
of a dirty bulb. Near him, a heap
of enameled pans as white as skulls
looms in the catacomb shadows,
and old toilets with dry red throats
cough up bouquets of curtain rods.

You've seen him somewhere before.
He's wearing the green leisure suit
you threw out with the garbage,
and the Christmas tie you hated,
and the ventilated wingtip shoes
you found in your father's closet
and wore as a joke. And the glasses
which finally fit him, through which
he looks to see you looking back—
two mirrors which flash and glance—
are those through which one day
you too will look down over the years,
when you have grown old and thin
and no longer particular,
and the things you once thought
you were rid of forever
have taken you back in their arms.

Camera

It's an old box camera,
a Brownie, the color and shape
of the battery out of a car,
but smaller, lighter.
All the good times—
the clumsy picnics on the grass,
the new Dodge,
the Easter Sundays—
each with its own clear instant
in the fluid of time,
all these have leaked away,
leaving this shell,
this little battery without a spark.

A Room in the Past

It's a kitchen. Its curtains fill
with a morning light so bright
you can't see beyond its windows
into the afternoon. A kitchen
falling through time with its things
in their places, the dishes jingling
up in the cupboard, the bucket
of drinking water rippled as if
a truck had just gone past, but that truck
was thirty years. No one's at home
in this room. Its counter is wiped,
and the dishrag hangs from its nail,
a dry leaf. In housedresses of mist,
blue aprons of rain, my grandmother
moved through this life like a ghost,
and when she had finished her years,
she put them all back in their places
and wiped out the sink, turning her back
on the rest of us, forever.

In January, 1962

With his hat on the table before him,
my grandfather waited until it was time
to go to my grandmother's funeral.
Beyond the window, his eighty-eighth winter
lay white in its furrows. The little creek
which cut through his cornfield was frozen.
Past the creek and the broken, brown stubble,
on a hill which thirty years before
he'd given the town, a green tent flapped
under the cedars. Throughout the day before,
he'd stayed there by the window watching
the blue woodsmoke from the thawing-barrels
catch in the bitter wind and vanish,
and had seen, so small in the distance,
a man breaking the earth with a pick.
I suppose he could feel that faraway work
in his hands—the steel-smooth, cold oak handle;
the thick, dull shock at the wrists—
for the following morning, as we waited there,
it was as if it hurt him to move them,
those hard old hands which lay curled and still
near the soft gray felt hat on the table.

Tillage Marks

On this flat stone,
too heavy for one man alone
to pick up and carry
to the edge of his field,
are the faint white marks
of a plow, one plow
or many, the sharp blade
crisscrossing its face
like a lesson scratched there
in chalk, the same lesson
taught over and over,
to one man alone in his field
for fifty or sixty years,
or to fifty such men,
each alone, each plow striking
this stone, in this field
which he thought to be his.

A Child's Grave Marker

A small block of granite
engraved with her name and the dates
just wasn't quite pretty enough
for this lost little girl
or her parents, who added a lamb
cast in plaster of paris,
using the same kind of cake mold
my grandmother had—iron,
heavy and black as a skillet.
The lamb came out coconut-white,
and seventy years have proven it
soft in the rain. On this hill,
overlooking a river in Iowa,
it melts in its own sweet time.

Father

—*Theodore Briggs Kooser*
May 19, 1902–December 31, 1979

You spent fifty-five years
walking the hard floors
of the retail business,
first, as a boy playing store

in your grandmother's barn,
sewing feathers on hats
that the neighbors threw out,
then stepping out onto

the smooth pine planks
of your uncle's grocery—
SALADA TEA in gold leaf
over the door, your uncle

and father still young then
in handlebar mustaches,
white aprons with dusters
tucked into their sashes—

then to the varnished oak
of a dry goods store—
music to your ears,
that bumpety-bump

of bolts of bright cloth
on the counter tops,
the small rattle of buttons,
the bell in the register—

then on to the cold tile
of a bigger store, and then one
still bigger—gray carpet,
wide aisles, a new town

to get used to—then into
retirement, a few sales
in your own garage,
the concrete under your feet.

You had good legs, Dad,
and a good storekeeper's eye:
asked once if you remembered
a teacher of mine,

you said, "I certainly do;
size ten, a little something
in blue." How you loved
what you'd done with your life!

Now you're gone, and the clerks
are lazy, the glass cases
smudged, the sale sweaters
pulled off on the floor.

But what good times we had
before it was over:
after those stores had closed,
you posing as customers,

strutting in big flowered hats,
those aisles like a stage,
the pale manikins watching;
we laughed till we cried.

At Midnight

Somewhere in the night,
a dog is barking,
starlight like beads of dew
along his tight chain.
No one is there
beyond the dark garden,
nothing to bark at
except, perhaps, the thoughts
of some old man
sending his memories
out for a midnight walk,
a rich cape
woven of many loves
swept recklessly
about his shoulders.

Central

As fine a piece of furniture
as any Steinway, all oak
and nickel and Bakelite,
her switchboard stood in the kitchen
stretching the truth. While she sat
with her ear to the valley,
rumor reached its red tendrils
from socket to socket, from farm
to farm. When the sun went down,
she sat in the dark. Those voices
she'd listened to all afternoon,
clear as the high sharp cries of geese,
flew over the house and were gone.
The loose lines buzzed. In the moonlight,
her hands held the wilted bouquets
of pink rubber. "Central," she'd say
to the darkness, "This is Central.
Hello? Is there anyone there?"

The Fan in the Window

It is September, and a cool breeze
from somewhere ahead is turning the blades;
night, and the slow flash of the fan
the last light between us and the darkness.
Dust has begun to collect on the blades,
haymaker's dust from distant fields,
dust riding to town on the night-black wings
of the crows, a thin frost of dust
which clings to the fan in just the way
we cling to the earth as it spins.
The fan has brought us through,
its shiny blades like the screw of a ship
that has pushed its way through summer—
cut flowers awash in its wake,
the stagnant Sargasso Sea of July
far behind us. For the moment, we rest,
we lie in the dark hull of the house,
we rock in the troughs off the shore
of October, the engine cooling,
the fan blades so lazily turning, but turning.

Myrtle

Wearing her yellow rubber slicker,
Myrtle, our *Journal* carrier,
has come early through rain and darkness
to bring us the news.
A woman of thirty or so,
with three small children at home,
she's told me she likes
a long walk by herself in the morning.
And with pride in her work,
she's wrapped the news neatly in plastic—
a bread bag, beaded with rain,
that reads WONDER.
From my doorway I watch her
flicker from porch to porch as she goes,
a yellow candle flame
no wind or weather dare extinguish.

Daddy Longlegs

Here, on fine long legs springy as steel,
a life rides, sealed in a small brown pill
that skims along over the basement floor
wrapped up in a simple obsession.
Eight legs reach out like the master ribs
of a web in which some thought is caught
dead center in its own small world,
a thought so far from the touch of things
that we can only guess at it. If mine,
it would be the secret dream
of walking alone across the floor of my life
with an easy grace, and with love enough
to live on at the center of myself.

Good-bye

You lean with one arm out
against the porch post,
your big hand cupping its curve,
shy of that handshake
we both know is coming.
And when we've said enough,
when the last small promises
begin to repeat, your eyes
come to mine, and then
you offer your hand,
dusted with chalk from the post,
and sticky with parting.

The Giant Slide

Beside the highway, the Giant Slide
with its rusty undulations lifts
out of the weeds. It hasn't been used
for a generation. The ticket booth
tilts to that side where the nickels shifted
over the years. A chain link fence keeps out
the children and drunks. Blue morning glories
climb halfway up the stairs, bright clusters
of laughter. Call it a passing fancy,
this slide that nobody slides down now.
Those screams have all gone east
on a wind that will never stop blowing
down from the Rockies and over the plains,
where things catch on for a little while,
bright leaves in a fence, and then are gone.

A Roadside Shrine in Kansas

Sunk into the earth
end up,
as if it had fallen
white as a comet
from heaven,
this bathtub,
clenching its claws
into fists,
now shelters
a Virgin
of plaster,
while through
the rusty drain hole,
one kneeling there
can see
in the shimmering distance,
God
walking the bean rows.

Decoration Day

It takes the hard work
of a dozen ants
to open each bud
of a peony.
For weeks, there they are,
clickety-clack,
biting the sutures
and licking the glue.
Then, one by one
on Decoration Day,
the blossoms explode,
tossing the ants
all over the yard.
Early that morning,
we find these flowers
opened, pink and white,
and in the wet grass,
hundreds of ants
with the staggers, all
watching the sky.

A Monday in May

It rained all weekend,
but today the peaked roofs
are as dusty and warm
as the backs of old donkeys
tied in the sun.
So much alike are our houses,
our lives. Under every eave—
leaf, cobweb, and feather;
and for each front yard
one sentimental maple,
who after a shower has passed,
weeps into her shadow
for hours.

A Buffalo Skull

No fine white bone-sheen now;
a hundred hard years
have worn it away, this stump
washed up on a bar
in the river, its horns
like broken roots,
its muzzle filled with sand
and the thin gray breath
of spider webs. Once,
they covered the grasslands
like the shadows of clouds,
and now the river gives up
just one skull, a hive of bone
like a fallen wasp's nest,
heavy, empty, and
full of the whine of the wind
and old thunder.

Laundry

A pink house trailer,
scuffed and rusted, sunken
in weeds. On the line,

five pale blue workshirts
up to their elbows
in raspberry canes—

a good, clean crew
of pickers, out early,
sleeves wet with dew,

and near them, a pair
of bright yellow panties
urging them on.

The Mouse

On the floor of a parking garage
I found a dead mouse. It was winter,
the world gone gray outside and in,
and the mouse a part of all that drabness—
the smallest part. He stood
like a windup mouse run down at last
but still on its wheels, a fast run
just behind him, and he'd pulled
his paws up tightly under his chin
as if he'd stopped to sniff at the edge
of something important—a mousehole maybe,
right under his nose and opening
out of the world. His back was arched
against entering there, and every muscle
had frozen in place like a spring.

Ladder

Against the low roof of a house
in the suburbs, someone has left
a ladder leaning, an old wooden ladder
too heavy to take down at night
and put up in the morning, the kind
that reaches beyond such a roof
by a good six feet, punching up
into the sky. The kind with paint
from another world on its rungs,
the cream and butter colored spots
from another time, the kind that
before you get up in the morning
knocks hard at the front of your house
like a sheriff, that stands there
in front of your door with a smile;
a ladder with solid authority,
with its pantlegs pressed, a ladder
that if it could whistle would whistle.

Walking at Noon Near the
Burlington Depot in Lincoln, Nebraska

—to the memory of James Wright

On the rat-gray dock
of the candy factory,
workers in caps and aprons
as white as divinity
sit on their heels and smoke
in the warm spring sunlight
thick with butterscotch.

In the next block down,
outside a warehouse,
its big doors rolled and bolted
over the dusty hush
of pyramids of cartons,
two pickets in lettered vests
call back and forth, their voices
a clatter of echoes.

A girl sits in her car,
an old tan Oldsmobile
broken down over its tires,
and plays the radio.

On the grill of a semi
smelling of heat and distance,
one tattered butterfly.

And an empty grocery cart
from Safeway, miles from here,
leans into its reflection
in a blackened window, a little
piano recital of chrome
for someone to whom all things
were full of sadness.

A Patch of Sunlight

Over the old dog's eye,
the blue cloud
of a cataract.
Along one leg, a tremor—
some tiny animal
running in long brown grass.

Carp

On the river bottom,
the carp have blown out
all the candles.

They whisper along
over the closed, black
bibles of clams.

Water-monks these,
with mouths like those
of angels singing,

but not angelic,
so very naked now
in darkness,

their cool, hard bodies
touching, among
the tapestries of weed.

At the Center

In Kansas, on top
of an old piano,
a starfish, dry
as a fancy pastry
left sitting there
during a wedding,
spreads its brown arms
over the foam
of a white lace doily,
reaching for water
in five directions.

A Sunset

The steeple so carefully
swings its long shadow
over the grass that the bell's
small shadow does not ring,
nor do the soft gray shadows
of its pigeons fly. Light
rises into the treetops
like the bubbles in beer.
A man walks home alone,
his shadow, shambling ahead,
some dark old woman
who rents out rooms.
She's wrapped in a shawl
that hides her face
in folds of blackness,
and closed in her fist
is the evening star.

The Ride

—to the memory of John Gardner

High in the night, we rock, we rock in the stars
while the Ferris wheel stops to let someone off
in the darkness below, someone we saw there
a half turn ahead of us, riding alone,
a man with white hair who threw up his hands
going down. We were too frightened for that.
We held on with both hands as we followed him,
climbing and falling, around and around,
while the world turned beneath us, rolled under
the wheel with its music, its flickering lights.
Now we rock in the starlight. Beneath us,
the music has stopped, the motor pops at idle.
The midway goes dark, booth to booth, as he passes.

At Nightfall

In feathers the color of dusk, a swallow,
up under the shadowy eaves of the barn,
weaves now, with skillful beak and chitter,
one bright white feather into her nest
to guide her flight home in the darkness.
It has taken a hundred thousand years
for a bird to learn this one trick with a feather,
a simple thing. And the world is alive
with such innocent progress. But to what
safe place shall any of us return
in the last smoky nightfall,
when we in our madness have put the torch
to the hope in every nest and feather?

At the Office Early

Rain has beaded the panes
of my office windows,
and in each little lens
the bank at the corner
hangs upside down.
What wonderful music
this rain must have made
in the night, a thousand banks
turned over, the change
crashing out of the drawers
and bouncing upstairs
to the roof, the soft
percussion of ferns
dropping out of their pots,
the ball-point pens
popping out of their sockets
in a fluffy snow
of deposit slips.
Now all day long,
as the sun dries the glass,
I'll hear the soft piano
of banks righting themselves,
the underpaid tellers
counting their nickels and dimes.

Cleaning a Bass

She put it on the chopping block
and it flopped a little, the red rick-rack
of its sharp gills sawing the evening air
into lengths, its yellow eyes like glass,
like the eyes of a long-forgotten doll
in the light of an attic. "They feel no pain,"
she told me, setting the fish upright,
and with a chunk of stovewood
she drove an ice pick through its skull
and into the block. The big fish curled
on its pin like a silver pennant
and then relaxed, but I could see life
in those eyes, which stared at the darkening
world of the air with a terrible wonder.
"It's true," she said, looking over at me
through the gathering shadows, "they feel no pain,"
and she took her Swedish filleting knife
with its beautiful blade that leaped and flashed
like a fish itself, and with one stroke
laid the bass bare to its shivering spine.

An Empty Shotgun Shell

It's a handsome thing
in its uniform—
all crimson and brass—
standing guard
at the gate to the field,
but something
is wrong at its heart.
It's dark in there,
so dark a whole night
could squeeze in,
could shrink back up in there
like a spider,
a black one
with smoke in its hair.

A Quarter Moon Just Before Dawn

There's sun on the moon's back
as she stoops to pick up
a star that she's dropped in her garden.
And stars keep falling,
through little holes in the bottoms
of her sweater pockets.
She's stretched them out
by hiding her hands all these years—
big peasant's hands
with night under their nails.

A Letter

I have tried a dozen ways
to say those things
and have failed: how the moon
with its bruises
climbs branch over branch
through the empty tree;
how the cool November dusk,
like a wind, has blown
these old gray houses up
against the darkness;
and what these things
have come to mean to me
without you. I raked the yard
this morning, and it rained
this afternoon. Tonight,
along the shiny street,
the bags of leaves—
wet-shouldered
but warm in their skins—
are huddled together, close
so close to life.

Latvian Neighborhood

Along this street,
snow blows
from the shoulders
of old houses,
lifts,
catches the wind
like long white hair,
like pipe smoke,
like the thin gray scarves
of immigrants
standing in line,
hands in their pockets,
cold fingers
pinching the lint
of their stories.

The Voyager II Satellite

The tin man is cold;
the glitter of distant worlds
is like snow on his coat.
Free-falling through space,
he spreads his arms
and slowly turns,
hands reaching to catch
the white, elusive
dandelion fuzz
of starlight. He is the dove
with wings of purest gold
sent out upon the deep
to seek a place for us,
the goat upon whose back
we've sent our problems
into exile, the dreamy beast
of peace and science
who now grows smaller, smaller,
falling so gracefully
into the great blank face
of God.

The Witness

The divorce judge has asked for a witness,
and you wait at the back of the courtroom
as still as a flag on its stand, your best dress
falling in smooth, even folds that begin now
to gather the dust of white bouquets
which like a veil of lace is lifting
away from the kiss of the sunlit windows.

In your lap, where you left them, your hands
lie fallen apart like the rinds of a fruit.
Whatever they cupped has been eaten away.
Beyond you, across a lake of light
where years have sunk and settled to the floor,
the voices drone on with the hollow sound
of boats rubbing a dock that they're tied to.

You know what to say when they call you.

As the President Spoke

As the President spoke, he raised a finger
to emphasize something he said. I've forgotten
just what he was saying, but as he spoke
he glanced at that finger as if it were
somebody else's, and his face went slack and gray,
and he folded his finger back into his hand
and put it down under the podium
along with whatever it meant, with whatever he'd seen
as it spun out and away from that bony axis.

The Pitch

Tight on the fat man's wrist
is a watch with a misty face.
His hand is hot on your sleeve.
He wants you to give him a minute,

friend, of your precious time.
He's got something for you
and the little lady. Call it
security, call it insurance,

call it aluminum siding.
Subscribe to these six magazines
and the fat man wins a nice trip
to Hawaii, friend, a nice trip

to Acapulco. A fat man
hasn't much time in this world.
His pulse has one foot in a cast.
On his cheeks, red cobwebs appear.

He's got the Moose Lodge on his breath
like a vinegar bath, and his eyes
are yellow caution lights. Listen,
he's got a little woman, *too*.

The Sigh

You lie in your bed and sigh,
and the springs deep in the mattress
sing out with the same low note,
mocking your sadness. It's hard—
not the mattress, but life.
Life is hard. All along
you thought you could trust in
your own bed, your own sorrow.
You thought you were sleeping alone.

The Onion Woman

All of the clothes she owns
she wears in layers, coat
upon coat upon coat
like an onion. She's wrapped
the woman inside, the taste
of the woman, her odors,
her heart. But the fear
still shows through all those skins—
that tight white core
where the shoot has withered.

Hobo Jungle

A fat brown car seat, mushy with rain.
A few fire-blackened cans. A bucket
without any bottom but holding
a full measure of cottonwood leaves.
Not much of a story. You've heard it all
time and again—a few rusty words
enclosing a center of darkness, an edge
that can cut if you try prying the lid.

An August Night

High in the trees, cicadas weave
a wickerwork of longing.
In the shadows between two houses,
a man peers into a room
through the hum of a window fan,
the fragrance of his hair oil
like distant music, far too faint
to awaken the naked girl
on the clean linen of moonlight.

The Urine Specimen

In the clinic, a sun-bleached shell of stone
on the shore of the city, you enter
the last small chamber, a little closet
chastened with pearl—cool, white, and glistening—
and over the chilly well of the toilet
you trickle your precious sum in a cup.
It's as simple as that. But the heat
of this gold your body's melted and poured out
into a form begins to enthrall you,
warming your hand with your flesh's fevers
in a terrible way. It's like holding
an organ—spleen or fatty pancreas,
a lobe from your foamy brain still steaming
with worry. You know that just outside
a nurse is waiting to cool it into a gel
and slice it onto a microscope slide
for the doctor, who in it will read your future,
wringing his hands. You lift the chalice and toast
the long life of your friend there in the mirror,
who wanly smiles, but does not drink to you.

Geronimo's Mirror

That flash from a distant hillside,
that firefly in the blue shadows of rock—
that's Geronimo's mirror.
After all of these years, he's up there
still trying to warn us
that the soldiers are coming.
He sees them riding along the horizon
in an endless line,
sees them dipping down into the valley
rider by rider.
His mirror of tin, cupped in his palm,
says they're nearer now.
It says he can hear the black rock
sounding under their hooves,
can smell the sharp smoke of dust in the air.
Now he can hear their dark voices,
the old voices of horses,
and the talk that is leather's.
And now they are climbing the hill,
that holy hill that is Geronimo's,
but he is not afraid.
His mirror is warning the others,
and we are the others.

Porch Swing in September

The porch swing hangs fixed in a morning sun
that bleaches its gray slats, its flowered cushion
whose flowers have faded, like those of summer,
and a small brown spider has hung out her web
on a line between porch post and chain
so that no one may swing without breaking it.
She is saying it's time that the swinging were done with,
time that the creaking and pinging and popping
that sang through the ceiling were past,
time now for the soft vibrations of moths,
the wasp tapping each board for an entrance,
the cool dewdrops to brush from her work
every morning, one world at a time.